MW01601406

ISBN: 9798316916092

Dedication

I dedicate this book to my beloved spouse, James McLean, with whom I pray daily. Your unwavering faith and love strengthen my prayer life and inspire me to seek God's presence with you every day.

To my dear mother, who first taught me the power of prayer. You reminded me that a family that prays together stays together, and your example has shaped my heart and spirit in ways words can scarcely express.

To my children and grandchildren, may you always cherish the power of prayer and know that it is never too early or too late to seek God with your whole heart.

And to my church family, whose support, prayers, and fellowship encourage me to keep praying without ceasing. You are a constant reminder that prayer works —changing our hearts, our lives, and the world around us.

Prayer changes things. It changes us, and it changes others.

Prayer Focus - Table of Contents

PRAYERS FOR THE
GOOD FIGHT

Persistent Faith in Action

JENNIFER MCLEAN

Prayer One

PERSISTENT IN PRAYER

Honoring God Through Our Faith & Dependence

Persistent prayer honors God because it demonstrates our complete dependence on Him. In Hebrews 11:6, we are reminded, *"But without faith, it is impossible to please Him: for he that cometh to God must believe that He is and that He is a rewarder of them that diligently seek Him."* When we persistently pray, we declare our trust in God, acknowledging that He is both our provider and our rewarder.

Prayer as Communication: Asking, Seeking, Knocking

In Matthew 7:7-11, Jesus invites us to engage in persistent prayer: *"Ask, and it shall be given you; seek, and ye shall find; knock, and it shall be opened unto you. For everyone that asketh receiveth; and he that seeketh findeth; and to him that knocketh it shall be opened."* Here, we see the three essential actions in prayer: asking, seeking, and knocking.

- **Asking** is the simple request, the direct communication of our needs and desires to God.
- **Seeking** is an active pursuit, seeking God's will and direction in our lives.
- **Knocking** represents our persistence—continuing to seek God's door, knowing He is faithful to answer.

Jesus uses the example of a father who gives his children good gifts to show us how much more our perfect and loving Heavenly Father will give to those who ask Him. God listens, we talk, and He responds—always with love and care.

The Persistent Widow: A Lesson in Perseverance
In Luke 18:2-8, Jesus shares the parable of the persistent widow. The widow, who kept coming to an unrighteous judge, never gave up on her pursuit for justice. She came day after day, and eventually, the judge granted her request, not because he cared for her but because her persistence wore him down.

Jesus tells us to "hear what the unrighteous judge says" and then contrasts that with the justice God will bring to His elect, who cry out to Him day and night. He asks, "Will He delay long over them?" Jesus promises, "I tell you, He will give justice to them speedily."

Just like the widow, we are called to persist in prayer. She didn't give up—she kept coming and got what she wanted because of her persistence. Persistence works on earth, and it works even more powerfully in heaven.

Prayer and God's Kingdom Resources
Through persistent prayer, I can tap into the abundant resources of God's Kingdom. When I consistently pray, I align myself with His will and invite His provision, guidance, and intervention into my life. Prayer is not just about asking for our needs to be met—it's a continual alignment with God's perfect plan for our lives.

Let me be like the widow in the parable: unyielding in my faith, unwavering in my trust, and persistent in pursuing God's Kingdom. God hears the cries of His people, and He responds to those who seek Him diligently.

As we persist in prayer, let us remember that God is faithful. He rewards those who seek Him with a heart of faith. Prayer is an act of relationship—both speaking and listening, asking and receiving. It is a powerful tool that taps into God's limitless resources; through it, we partner with Him to bring His will to earth.

Prayer Two

PRAYER OF REPENTANCE

Heavenly Father,

I come before You with a humble and contrite heart, acknowledging that I have sinned against You in thought, word, and deed. I confess my sins, Lord, and I ask for Your forgiveness. I recognize that I have fallen short of Your glory.

I repent for the things I have done in rebellion, for the things I have neglected, and for the ways I have hurt others and dishonored You. I ask You to cleanse me from all unrighteousness and purify me from every defilement. Wash me clean by the precious blood of Jesus Christ.

I repent of the times I have acted out of selfishness, pride, anger, jealousy, and unforgiveness. I lay these sins before You, asking You to remove them from my heart and fill me with Your peace, love, and grace. Restore me, Lord, to a right relationship with You, and help me to walk in Your ways.

I forgive those who have wronged me as You have forgiven me. In obedience to Your Word, I choose to release all bitterness, resentment, and unforgiveness from my heart. Help me, Lord, to love as You love and to show compassion and mercy to others, just as You have shown me.

I also repent for the times I have failed to trust You fully or to step out in faith. I surrender my will to You, asking for Your guidance, strength, and wisdom to follow Your path. Transform my heart and mind and lead me in the way everlasting.

Thank You, Lord, for Your new grace and mercy every morning. I trust in Your unfailing love, and I believe that I am forgiven through the sacrifice of Your Son, Jesus Christ. Help me to walk in Your righteousness, and empower me by Your Holy Spirit to live a life that brings honor and glory to Your name.

In Jesus' name, I pray,
Amen.

Prayer Three

PRAYER FOR GREAT GRACE

Lord, Anoint Me with Great Grace.

Lord, I come before You, asking that You help me bring honor to You. I thank You that I walk in victory through Christ Jesus.

Help me live a life of repentance, fully surrendered to You, Father. Grant me the Spirit of Wisdom and revelation, giving me ever-increasing insight and foresight.

Give me the wisdom of the ant, as described in Proverbs 6:6-8 (Voice Bible):

"Take a lesson from the ant, you who love leisure and ease. Observe how it works, and dare to be just as wise. It has no boss, no one laying down the law or telling it what to do, yet it gathers its food through summer and takes what it needs from the harvest."

Holy Spirit, mature me and take me from glory to glory.

In the mighty name of Jesus, let every relationship damaged by demonic interference be restored. Lord, equip me for such a time as this, and I thank You for an end-time anointing.

Let me be Your agent here on Earth.

Help me to love others and not fight against them.
Let love permeate through me, and may I continually die to myself in the mighty name of Jesus.
Lord, take me from the pit to the palace.
Holy Spirit, I yield my lips, eyes, and ears to You.
I speak crop failure on every idle word spoken.

Let me walk in unity as the body of Christ, as Hebrews 10:25 (Voice Bible) reminds me: *"Not forgetting to gather as a community, as some have forgotten, but encouraging each other, especially as the day of His return approaches."*

I recognize that assembling isn't just for church services but also in small groups, on calls, on Zoom, and through social media.

The key is gathering with fellow believers. Your Word declares that one can put a thousand to flight, and two can put ten thousand to flight—there's power in agreement.

At this hour, it is critical that I do not forsake the assembly. In doing so, I will be strengthened and protected.

I declare that the dangers of isolation—discouragement, doubt, and division—will not take root in me.

As 1 Peter 5:8 warns, *"Be vigilant because your adversary, the devil, walks about seeking whom he may devour."*

I recognize that the enemy preys on isolation. Psalm 133:1 reminds me, *"Behold, how good and how pleasant it is for brethren to dwell together in unity."*

Lord, I plead for unity to prevail among my children, your churches, and our leaders. United I stand, but divided I fall. Unite me, O God, by the power of Your Spirit.

Bind me with cords of love and unity that cannot be broken. I command every wall of division to fall flat, just as the walls of Jericho did.

Lord, arouse Your church deeply for the lost and perishing. Give me an intense burden and passion to rescue men, women, boys, and girls from the flames of hell.

Awaken me to a higher standard of holiness and godliness, for without holiness, no one shall see You.

Help me to love others sincerely, from the heart. May I be my brother's keeper, seeking the good of others, and may Your love flow freely through me.

In Jesus' name, I pray.
Amen.

Prayer Four

PRAYER FOR
HEALTH & HEALING

Father,

I come before You, interceding for health and healing in my life. I stand in the authority You've given me and intercept every projection of the enemy against my body and mind. Let healing angels minister to my body, restoring every area of need and to those I am standing in the gap for. You are the Great Physician, and I trust in Your divine power to heal.

In the name of Jesus, I command every spirit of death attempting to steal my life to lose its grip and let go. I declare that I shall live and not die, and I will boldly proclaim the works of the Lord.

I claim the healing power of Jesus' stripes. He bore my sicknesses and infirmities on the cross, and I firmly believe that His resurrection power is at work in my body today.

I am shielded and covered by Your angels, and no sickness, disease, or virus can penetrate my atmosphere. Surround me with Your glory, Lord.

I cast out every spirit of infirmity attacking my body in the mighty name of Jesus.

I break, rebuke, and cast out any spirit of cancer attempting to establish itself in my blood, skin, lungs, bones, breasts, throat, back, spine, liver, colon, kidneys, or any part of my body.

I come against breathing problems, autoimmune diseases, arthritis, lupus, Alzheimer's, anxiety, and insomnia in the name of Jesus, rejecting their hold on me.

I speak healing and strength to my bones, muscles, joints, and organs.

I release myself from all heart attacks rooted in fear, and I command every spirit of fear to leave in Jesus' name. I release myself from the grip of diabetes and high blood pressure rooted in self-hatred and inheritance.

I declare that I am fearfully and wonderfully made. Let my body function according to Your perfect design, Father. I invite healing encounters in my dreams.

I speak to every variant of COVID and every respiratory disease, commanding them to dry up upon contact. I bind the effects of COVID-19 and any adverse impacts from vaccines or medication.

Father, strengthen my immune system and protect me from all harm.

I am shielded and protected by Jesus' blood, and I claim Your unwavering divine protection over my health.

In Jesus' name, I pray.
Amen.

Prayer Five

PRAYER FOR THE PEACE OF ISRAEL

Father, I come before You, lifting Israel in prayer.

May peace be within her walls and prosperity within her palaces. Lord, send Your peace to Israel and dispatch Your angelic guardians and mighty warrior battalions to surround her. Protect Israel from those who seek to devour and destroy, hiding her safely in the shelter of Your presence. You, Lord, keep her safe from the schemes of the enemy and the accusations of deceitful tongues.

I ask that You nullify the plans of ungodly nations who rise against Israel, making their counsel ineffective. As Your Word declares, no witchcraft can succeed against Israel (Numbers 23:23).

There is no enchantment or omen against Jacob and no divination against Israel. At the appointed time, all will know what You, O God, have done for Your people.

Father, I pray that Israel will be protected from any ungodly alliances with nations seeking to entrap her. I ask that You send Your divine protection over Israel's borders, with blood bombs and missiles forming a protective shield around her.

I lift every soldier, every hostage, and every individual in Israel's care. I pray for the safe release of every hostage in the mighty name of Jesus. Lion of Judah, roar!

Let Your power and glory be seen in this hour. I decree Your protection over Israel as I decree Psalm 91 over the land, knowing You are her refuge, fortress, and deliverer.

May Israel trust in You for her security and protection. Father, I declare that You will receive all the glory. You will show up strong and faithful in this time of need.

In the mighty name of Jesus, Amen.

Prayer Six

PRAYER FOR THE POLITICAL CLIMATE IN AMERICA

Heavenly Father,

I come before You, humbling myself as Your child, called by Your name.

I decree that the United States of America yields to You.

I ask that You patrol every area of this nation, binding the works of the enemy and covering ever individual, every community, and every corner of the land.

Show Your strength, might, and goodness over this nation, releasing miracles that reveal to all that You are God.

Lord, expose every plan and purpose of the enemy against this land.

In the name of Jesus, I stand in the gap for the leaders of this nation—our communities, cities, states, and regions. I plead the precious blood of Jesus over every appointed and elected position.

I pray for the people's minds that they may be freed from the enemy's influence, severing all connections to the prince of the power of the air. I ask You to break every chain, allowing principalities, powers, rulers of darkness, and spiritual wickedness to control my generation's offices and positions of influence.

Your Word says that when godly men reign, the people rejoice.

Father, deliver me from the oppression of the ungodly in high places.

Have mercy on this nation for the abominations in the land.

I repent for the sins of my forefathers and my generation.

Forgive us for any laws or actions that build Babylonian strongholds through perversion and the bloodshed of the innocent. I ask that vengeance be Yours, O God.

Let Your Holy Spirit expose and deal with every hidden agenda within our leadership. I pray against every political pursuit that prioritizes the rich while neglecting the poor and preys upon the needy through deceptive systems and agendas.

Father, I pray for the White House, the Capitol, and every leader in this nation. I ask for wisdom to rest upon them. Protect the president and his family from sabotage, conspiracies, terrorist attacks, and any attacks on their lives. Let the blood of Jesus cover them.

May Your blessings overflow from the highest position in the land, bringing wisdom, favor, and protection.

I ask that leaders live peaceable lives ruled by the fear of the Lord.

Let them lead with wisdom, understanding, and a heart to serve the people.

I pray that the leaders of this nation will bow before You and serve You with all their hearts.

I declare that Your Kingdom comes, and Your will is done on earth as in heaven.

I pray for revival, especially on Capitol Hill, to transform this nation.

Let our leaders tremble at the presence of the Lord and hear the Word of the Lord. Open doors so that your word will be proclaimed.

Raise leaders who will bless this nation's families, and let Your glory fill the land.

I also pray for the salvation of all leaders.
Open their hearts to the true and living God.
Let them come to know Jesus Christ as Lord and Savior.
Father, I pray for repentance that will bring healing to the land. Deliver our nation and its leaders.

I ask for a new spirit of leadership that breaks covenants with death and seeks righteousness.

Let every veil of deception be destroyed, and let the truth of Your Word prevail.

I decree that laws reflecting Your will be passed.

I pray for the economy's healing as You raise leaders who will steward this nation wisely.

Let Your blessings flow through the land, bringing justice, peace, and prosperity.

I decree that America is the inheritance of the Lord, and the Kingdom belongs to Jesus Christ.

Every political leader, from the president to every council member, is subject to Your authority.

I declare Jesus is Lord over America!

I declare that no weapon formed against this nation shall prosper, and every plan of terrorism, sabotage, or corruption is nullified.

In the name of Jesus, I decree that my country is under the governance of the Lord God Almighty.

In Jesus' mighty name, I pray.
Amen.

Prayer Seven

PRAYER FOR SALVATION

Father in Heaven,

I pray for lost people who need Your saving grace. Lord, you are the Way, the Truth, and the Life, and no one comes to the Father except through You (John 14:6). I pray that You would open the hearts and minds of those who do not yet know You.

I lift the lost souls of this world to You today—every man, woman, and child from here to the farthest corner of the earth. I intercede on their behalf, believing by faith that many, even today, will have the opportunity to accept Jesus as their Lord and Savior. I pray for souls to be brought from darkness into Your marvelous light.

I ask that You use me to bring people into Your Kingdom. Show me the harvest You are calling me to, and guide me to those who need to hear the Good News. I come against every spirit of darkness and bind the enemy's work, particularly the blinding spirit of the antichrist, that hinders people from coming to know You. I loose Your power to deliver deliverance and salvation to those ready to receive.

Holy Spirit, I ask that You convict them of their sin, draw them to Jesus, and reveal the overwhelming depth of His love and sacrifice on the cross. May they understand that Jesus died for their sins, was buried, and rose again, offering eternal life through faith in Him.

I pray that they will confess their need for a Savior, repent of their sins, and receive Jesus as their Lord and Savior. May they experience the overwhelming joy of knowing they are forgiven and deeply loved by You, and may their hearts be filled with the uncontainable joy of salvation.

Father, I ask that You place people in their lives who can speak Your truth and share Your love. Continue to pursue them with Your grace and mercy, opening their eyes to Your Kingdom's beauty and the hope found only in Jesus.

Thank You, Father, for Your relentless love and for the promise of salvation to all who call on the name of Jesus. I am grateful for the opportunity to be Your instrument in this divine mission.

In Jesus' name,
Amen.

Prayer Eight

PRAYER FOR REPENTANCE, HEALING, AND DIVINE PROTECTION

Father, as I come before you, I humble myself in your presence. I ask for Your forgiveness for all my sins, known and unknown. Forgive me, Lord, if I have borne false witness or wronged anyone. You, O Lord, are the potter, and I am the clay. Shape, mold, and transform me into a vessel that bring You glory.

Holy Spirit, you are the revealer of truth. I ask that You uncover anything in me that is not pleasing to You. Remove anything that hinders my prayers, and let my petitions be effective and powerful. Awaken me by Your Spirit, and help me to live daily by the strength You provide. Thank You for being my advocate, comforter, encourager, helper, and counselor. I praise You for Your protection and guidance, for You watch over and lead me with Your wisdom.

Lord, thank You for this new season. I ask You to detach me from the old and lead me into the new. Heal my emotions, my heart, and my past. Keep me saved, sanctified, and whole in Jesus' name. I renounce all old ties, soul ties, and fragments of my soul that bind me to the past. Restore me, Lord, and cover me with your precious blood.

In Jesus' name, I bind and command all hindering spirits of

distraction, ungodly attraction, confusion, and delusion to be removed from my life. I declare that I have the mind of Christ —the same mind that is in Christ Jesus is in me. I stand firm and focused on Your calling for my life.

I plead the blood of Jesus over my past—over every traumatic experience, every painful memory, every secret, every ill word spoken over me or my family, and every event that has seeded negativity in my heart. I place these under the blood of Jesus, trusting that You, Lord, will judge and heal. Every trespassing agent sent against our spiritual, mental, emotional, and physical well-being, I cast them out in Jesus' name. We are whole, from the top of our heads to the bottom of our feet.

I renounce every spirit assigned to me or my family through generations, associations, or incantations. I break every chain and dismiss every evil influence that seeks to bind us. We are under the divine protection of the Holy Spirit, and every territorial force sent to oppress us is covered by the blood of Jesus. We have a clear conscience, free from condemnation.

I thank You for inner healing. I know You care for us. I cast my cares upon You and rest in Your love and peace. Fill every empty place in my heart with Your presence, and help me to live in alignment with Your will. I am sanctified and satisfied with Your purpose for my life.

Let the gifts and fruit of the Spirit flow through me abundantly. May Your love, peace, patience, kindness, goodness, faith, gentleness, and self-control be evident in my life. I am steadfast and stable in my calling, and embrace the fullness of Your will for me.

Lord, I thank You for the power of Your Word. I claim the promises of Isaiah 54:13-17, knowing that no weapon formed against me shall prosper. I shall not be ashamed or confounded but will rise above every obstacle. I decree and declare that what the enemy meant for evil, you will turn for my good.

Father, let Your prophetic words over me come to fruition. I ask for divine favor and for Your scepter to extend toward me. I trust in Your provision, protection, and care for my ministries, family, finances, and work. I trust in Your love, knowing You are faithful in fulfilling Your promises.

Every evil altar raised against me is destroyed by fire in Jesus' name. I declare that any prayers or curses spoken against me shall fall to the ground. I stand in the authority You've given me and decree a season of acceleration, blessings, and divine alignment.

I decree restoration in every area of my life, that I am blessed going in and coming out, and that whatever I touch shall prosper. I declare that every hindrance is removed. I decree soundness of mind, emotional healing, and removing every negative influence.

Lord, thank You for divine relationships, placing me in the right place at the right time and aligning me with the people who will help me fulfill Your purpose. I believe You are shooting me into my destiny, and I walk by faith, knowing that You are with me every step. In Jesus' mighty name, we pray. Amen.

Prayer Nine

PRAYER AGAINST SPIRITUAL FORCES

Heavenly Father, I come before You, standing firm in the power of Your might, knowing that my struggle is not against flesh and blood but against the rulers, authorities, and powers of this dark world and the spiritual forces of evil in the heavenly realms (Eph. 6:12). I boldly pull down every cosmic demonic power. I declare that every evil altar with my name upon it is set on fire and consumed in the mighty Name of Jesus. I decree judgment on every evil altar, rendering it powerless.

Father, help me never to erect demonic altars in my life. I renounce every agreement with the enemy and refuse to allow any foothold for the forces of darkness to operate in my life.

In the name of Jesus, I come against every storm orchestrated by the prince of the power of the air (Eph. 2:2). I cancel every storm and every work of the enemy now. I command the mega storms to weaken and dissipate, and I pray that lives would be spared and Your mercy would cover Your people.

I cancel every attempt to manipulate weather patterns through cloud seeding or other means. Let it fail every time, and let Your sovereign will prevail.

Father, purge me from all iniquity. I command all iniquity residing in my spirit, soul, body, bones, organs, blood, DNA, and genetic code to leave now in the Name of Jesus. I break every curse tied to these iniquities and declare that the righteousness of God is being established in my life. I claim Your blessings over me and my family in the mighty Name of Jesus. Amen.

Lord, let me walk in Your will. Cleanse me, Lord, and help me to remain clean and pure before You. Prepare me for Your return, and help me to stay humble. May I not be a godless believer but a faithful, repentant one. May the church awaken to repentance and rise with clean hands and a pure heart, forsaking every altar of darkness. Help me remain loyal to You, God.

Investigate my life, O Lord. Search me and know me. Cross examine and test me; reveal to me where I've gone wrong and guide me on the road to eternal life (Psalm 139:23-24, Message Bible).

Lord, I ask You to place a hedge of protection around me. Let nothing break the hedge You've placed around me. Keep me secure in Your protection, and help me never compromise for money or the things of this world. Keep my hands clean and my heart pure before You. I declare that I will fulfill everything written in my book. May my name be inscribed in the Book of Life, and may I walk in the fullness of the purpose You've called me to.

Lord, preserve me in Your mercy. I cry out for Your mercy today and ask that You speak to me more clearly. Help me discern Your voice; may I never follow a stranger's voice. I pray for the strength not to grow weary in the wait, trusting that everything will be made right in Your timing. In Jesus' mighty Name, I pray. Amen.

Prayer Ten

PRAYER FOR THE WISDOM OF GOD

Father God,

You said in Proverbs 4:7, wisdom is the principal thing; therefore, get wisdom, and with all thy getting, get understanding.

You also said in James 1:15 that you will generously give it to me if I ask. I am asking for wisdom. In these unprecedented times, I need Your wisdom more than ever. I need Your wisdom to guide my heart and mind. Grant me the discernment to see things as You do and the understanding to walk in the paths You have set before me. With faith, courage, and trust in Your perfect will.

Help me to lean not on my understanding but to trust in Your timing and seek Your guidance in every decision, Whether great or small. May Your wisdom lead me to peace. May it shine through my actions so that others might see Your goodness and truth reflected in me.

Fill me with Your Holy Spirit, That I may grow in knowledge and understanding, And live a life that testifies to Your eternal wisdom.

In Jesus' name, I pray.
Amen.

Prayer Eleven

PRAYER FOR SINGLES

Heavenly Father,

We come before You today with grateful hearts, trusting in Your perfect plan for our lives. Thank You for the gift of singleness, for the time it offers to grow closer to You, discover more of who You've created us to be, and build our lives on the foundation of Your love.

Lord, we pray for every single person so that they may find their identity and worth in You alone. Help them to fully embrace this season of life, knowing that it is not a time of lack but of purpose and preparation. Fill their hearts with peace, contentment, and joy as they trust You to lead them in every step.

Father, we ask that You guide their desires and prayers, aligning them with Your will. Whether You call them to marriage or a season of singleness, may they find fulfillment in Your purpose for them? Give them patience as they wait for Your timing, and help them to seek You above all else.

Lord, protect their hearts from loneliness and doubt. Remind them of Your constant presence, that You are with them always, and that they are never truly alone. Heal any past wounds or disappointments, and fill them with Your love, knowing it is sufficient and unchanging.

We pray for the right relationships to come into their lives in Your perfect timing—friendships that encourage, uplift, and strengthen them. If it is Your will for them to marry, bring them a partner who shares their heart for You, someone who will walk alongside them in faith and love.

Until then, help them to live in purpose and serve You with all their hearts, knowing that You have great plans for their future. May their lives shine with the love of Christ, and may they be vessels of Your grace and truth wherever they go.

Thank You, Lord, for Your faithfulness. We trust that You are preparing them for the next chapter, and we rest in Your perfect timing.

In Jesus' name, we pray. Amen.

Prayer Twelve

PRAYER FOR DIRECTION AND DELIVERANCE

Heavenly Father, Holy Spirit, open my spiritual eyes and ears so that I may hear and see clearly what You are revealing to me. Align my thoughts with Yours and let my ways reflect Your perfect will.

Father, grant me the anointing of Issachar, so I may discern the times and know precisely what to do in this season. I choose to move according to Your timing, trusting that You are always ahead of me.

Lord, I thank You for fighting my battles. I declare that I will not walk in weariness but in Your peace. I stand firm in my heavenly identity, knowing I am Your child, walking in my kingdom inheritance. Position me, Father, to enter my wealthy place. I trust that my seeds will sustain me, and I believe You will bring about a great recompense.

I command every Pharaoh spirit that seeks to hinder, harass, or delay Your blessings to be drowned by the power of the Holy Spirit.

I decree that my storehouses are blessed and declare Your mercy and protection over my life. I trust that every evil ruling against me will be overruled in the courtroom of heaven in the mighty name of Jesus.

Father, open the eyes of my heart so that I may become more aware of the spiritual battles surrounding me. Awaken me by the power of Your Holy Spirit to be watchful, sober-minded, and intentional in choosing righteousness. Grant me discernment to recognize the enemy's tactics and equip me to stand firm in Your truth.

I pray that a spirit of prayer and repentance be poured upon the Church, that we may be restored to You and fully walk in Your purpose. Keep me, O Lord, from the hands of the wicked. Preserve my family and me from violent men who seek to make my steps stumble. Expose, root out, and overthrow the plans of evil, in Jesus' name.

I stand against mass shootings, terrorist attacks, wars, domestic violence, and police brutality. I release unity in the name of Jesus. Thank You, Lord, that through Your death on the cross, you disarmed the powers of evil. Send forth Your light and truth, O Lord, to reveal the deeds of darkness and expose the plans of violence and murder.

By the power of Your Holy Spirit, convict those who have allowed their minds to be dominated by evil. Lead them to true repentance so that they may experience Your new life and rejoice in Your forgiving love.

Father, I stand in the gap for those struggling with suicidal thoughts. Help them find their way back to Your light. Let Your light shine in the darkness, dispelling hopelessness. Show them they are enough, and fill them with Your love and peace.

In Jesus' mighty name, I pray. Amen.

Prayer Thirteen

PRAYER FOR FINANCIAL BLESSINGS

Heavenly Father,

I thank You for redeeming the time for me. I am the righteousness of God in Christ Jesus, walking in Your statutes and keeping Your commandments. I declare that man's economy does not bind me; I am under the covering of the economy of God. I declare prosperity into my life, declaring that I have more coming in than going out. The spirit of lack, represented by the python spirit, is forever broken off from all my affairs.

Wherever the soles of my feet tread, the land is mine. Whatever I put my hands to will prosper. The wealth of the wicked is stored up for the righteous, and I am positioned to receive it. Blessings are running me down and overtaking me! Lord, I will enter into Your rest, and my enemies will flee before me.

My doorposts are covered with the precious blood of Jesus; with it, protection accompanies my financial increase. I declare that I will experience significant growth and enjoy the blessings that come with it.

I am so full of Your blessings, Lord, that I cannot help but share them. I am contagiously blessed. My field is blessed, my house is blessed, and the blessing of my heritage flows through my bloodline. I owe no man anything except love. I am a lender, not a borrower. I declare that I will be debt-free.

My mortgage and all properties will be paid in full, and my prosperity will be built on the foundation of love. I will not have to beg, borrow, or covet.

I declare the promise of Amos 9:13 (Message Bible):
"Things are going to happen so fast your head will swim, one thing fast on the heels of the other. You won't be able to keep up. Everything will be happening at once—and everywhere you look, blessings!"

Father, I thank You for blessing me beyond measure. I receive all that You have prepared for me and choose to walk in the fullness of Your abundance.

In Jesus' name, I pray.
Amen.

Prayer Fourteen

PRAYER POSTURES AND THEIR SIGNIFICANCE

These postures remind us that prayer is about our words and how we approach God's presence with our bodies, hearts, and minds.

- **On Your Knees – Eph. 3:14-19**
  - *"For this reason, I kneel before the Father, from whom every family in heaven and on earth derives its name."*
  - Kneeling in prayer represents humility and submission before God. It acknowledges God's greatness and our need for His grace. When we kneel, we physically posture ourselves in surrender, showing reverence and honor to the Lord.

- **In Your Bed – Ps. 63:6**
  - *"On my bed, I remember you; I think of you through the watches of the night."*
  - Prayer is not limited to specific times or places. When you can't sleep or lie down for rest, you can invite God into your thoughts in your bed. This posture reflects intimacy with God, even in quiet moments when the world is still. It's a place for reflection, praise, and surrender to His presence.

- **Out Loud – Ps. 142:1**
  - *"I cry aloud to the Lord; I lift up my voice to the Lord for mercy."*

- Speaking your prayers aloud is a powerful posture of declaration and urgency. It shows boldness and faith, declaring God's goodness and sovereignty over your situation. Out loud, we call on the Lord to hear our cries, knowing He listens attentively to our petitions.

- **Silent – 1 Sam. 1:12-13**
  - *"As she kept on praying to the Lord, Eli observed her mouth. Hannah was praying in her heart, and her lips were moving, but her voice was not heard."*
  - Sometimes, prayer is an internal dialogue with God. The silence in our hearts allows for deep connection, surrender, and listening. In these moments of quietness, God often speaks the loudest, and we allow Him to work in us without distractions.

- **Hands Lifted – 1 Tim. 2:8**
  - *"I want men everywhere to lift up holy hands in prayer, without anger or disputing."*
  - Lifting our hands in prayer is an outward sign of worship, surrender, and adoration. It's a gesture of openness and receptivity to God, acknowledging His power and authority. When we raise our hands, we offer ourselves fully to Him, ready to receive His blessings, guidance, and strength.

- **Eyes Open – John 17:1**
  - *"After Jesus said this, he looked toward heaven and prayed..."*
  - Sometimes, prayer is a gaze toward the heavens, fixing our eyes on God. Open eyes symbolize our focus on God's majesty, throne, and promises. In times of prayer, when we lift our eyes, we are reminded of His eternal perspective and the hope that comes from Him.

- **Head Bowed – Lam. 2:10**
  - *"The elders of the daughter of Zion sit on the ground in silence; they have sprinkled dust on their heads and girded themselves with sackcloth..."*
  - Bowing the head symbolizes mourning, humility, and repentance. It's an outward sign of our recognition of God's holiness and our own sinfulness, seeking His mercy and forgiveness. It can be a powerful expression of contrition and reverence in prayer.

- **Prostrate – Matt. 26:39**
  - *"Going a little farther, he fell with his face to the ground and prayed, 'My Father, if it is possible, may this cup be taken from me. Yet not as I will, but as you will.'"*
  - Prostrating oneself before God represents utter surrender and submission. It is an expression of total devotion, recognizing God's greatness and submitting to His will. Jesus, in His final moments before the cross, demonstrated this ultimate posture of surrender to the Father.

Prayer Fifteen

PRAYER FOR THE GENDER IDENTITY CRISIS

Father God, I come before You, lifting those who are struggling to reconcile their thoughts and desires with the gender of their birth. Lord, help me not to judge but to love them with Your unconditional love. I ask that You transform them from the inside out, revealing the root causes of their struggles. May they renounce the enemy's lies and embrace the truth that they are fearfully and wonderfully made by You, with a divine purpose as You created them to be.

Marvelous are Your works, Lord; my soul knows it very well. You have ordained men to be men and women to be women. I lift everyone struggling with their gender identity, and in Jesus' name, I ask that You send Holy and Godly wisdom into their lives through Your Spirit. I pray that You remove any evil agendas that seek to distort Your creation.

Teach every young boy to grow into a Godly man, full of holiness, sanctification, and purpose. Teach every young girl to grow into a mighty woman of God, set apart and sanctified, delighting in her femininity as Your beloved daughter. Help them to know that You created them perfectly in Your image, and they are to embrace and celebrate who they are.

Help every woman delight in her femininity, knowing that she is Your daughter and that You enjoy her unique, beautiful design. Help every man embrace his masculinity, knowing that he was born to be Your son and that You delight in him as such.

Lord, I ask that You protect them from the path of lies and destruction. Bring clarity about their birth gender and help them to embrace it fully. Protect them from wicked forces and evil agendas that seek to confuse them. As You placed an angel with a flaming sword in the Garden of Eden to guard the path of righteousness, place Your protection around them, guiding them away from confusion and harm. Let that angel turn them back from paths of unrighteousness and deceit.

Father, I cry out for mercy. Your Word says that when the enemy comes in like a flood, the Spirit of the Lord will raise a standard against him. The enemy has come like a flood with lies of gender confusion. I command the forces of the enemy to flee. Let every person, even those who do not yet know You, see the lies about gender for what they are—lies—and renounce them.

I rebuke the devourer on behalf of all affected by this wicked agenda and pray that You protect their hearts and minds from further deception. Strengthen their parents and loved ones to stand firm in Your truth and to pray with boldness and love.

In Jesus' name, I pray. Amen.

Prayer Sixteen

PRAYER OF BINDING AND LOOSING
(with Declarations of Victory)

Father, we come before You in the mighty name of Jesus Christ, acknowledging Your Word in Matthew 18:18, which declares that whatever we bind on earth will be bound in heaven, and whatever we lose on earth will be loosed in heaven. To bind is to restrict or restrain; to lose is to release or set free. We first bind Satan, every ruling spirit, and all principalities, powers, rulers of darkness, wicked spirits in high places, and every spirit not of the Holy Spirit. We bind them in all ways, manners, and forms, along with their seeds, works, plans, and activities directed at us, our spouse, children, family members, relatives, and all Christian believers.

We speak destruction upon every work, blueprint, plot, design, trap, snare, and assignment the enemy has set against us or our loved ones in any way, manner, or form. Father, Your Word promises that when the enemy comes in like a flood, Your Holy Spirit will raise a standard against them (Isaiah 59:19). Therefore, we decree that the Holy Spirit stops Satan and all his evil spirits dead in their tracks concerning us and our loved ones.

According to Job 22:28, Your Word says, *"Thou shalt also decree a thing, and it shall be established unto thee: and the light shall shine upon thy ways."*

Therefore, we decree and declare that all these prayers are accomplished and brought to pass, as we trust in faith and expectation in the mighty name of Jesus.

We Decree and Declare:
- No negative report shall dwell in our hearts or minds.
- We decree a tidal wave of miracles to be released.
- We decree recompense and that we shall recover all.
- We decree divine acceleration and divine activation.
- We decree supernatural increase, peace in our nation, and kingdom expansion.
- We decree new doors of opportunity and new keys of access.
- We decree that whatever we put our hands to will prosper.
- We decree kingdom marriages and greater blessings for married couples.
- We decree million-dollar ideas, strategies, and financial breakthroughs.
- We decree this is our season of NOW—New Ongoing Winnings. This is a season of victory, increase, and blessings.
- We decree double blessings—double joy, double opportunities, double favor, and double rewards for our trouble.
- We decree approvals, access granted, souls saved, healing, and deliverance.
- We decree that we are healthy and wealthy, and our families are healthy and wealthy.
- We decree that no weapon formed against us shall prosper.
- We decree debt cancellation and the supernatural receipt of titles and deeds.
- We declare that we will reap where we did not have to toil, in Jesus' name.

We Bind and Loosen:
We bind every word curse and every negative word spoken against us and our families, including words of condemnation, witchcraft, gossip, jealousy, backbiting, rebellion, racism, division, slothfulness, procrastination, religious spirits, greed, and poverty.

We loose deliverance, truth, holiness, unity, health, wealth, obedience, love, boldness, submission, the mind of Christ, and stability over our lives. Let our enemies be scattered, and let every fiery arrow of the enemy be extinguished. Let Your goodness and mercy follow us all the days of our lives.

A Final Decree of Divine Protection and Victory:
Let the Lord's shield be over us, guarding and protecting us from all harm. We thank You, Lord, for Your faithful protection, provision, and guidance. We trust in Your power, Your Word, and Your sovereignty. In the mighty name of Jesus Christ, we pray, believe, and receive all things in Jesus' Name, Amen.

Prayer Seventeen

PRAYER AGAINST MONITORING SPIRITS AND NEGATIVE INFLUENCES

Heavenly Father, in the mighty name of Jesus Christ, I come before You today with full authority and boldness. I bind every "watcher" agent, every "scanner" agent, every "tracker" agent, every "eavesdropper" agent, and every divinatory spirit that has been sent on assignment against me and my loved ones. I bind them now, along with all those in their chain of command, and cast them away from me in the name of Jesus.

I loose myself, my loved ones, and all we are and have from their influence and attacks. I declare that these prayers are already accomplished in the realm of the Holy Spirit. From this moment forward, these agents and spirits cannot see, hear, or understand my moves or words. They cannot track me, watch my activities, or follow my steps. I decree that their assignments are turned back upon themselves and will not prosper.

By the powerful Blood of Jesus Christ, I cancel the effects of all negative, witchcraft, and demonic dreams. I command every work of darkness and every negative influence upon my spirit, soul, body, life, family, and destiny to be nullified and erased forever in the name of Jesus Christ. I come against every power and principality, binding them by the Blood of the Lamb.

Every evil force that has sought to spoil my nights with fearful and disturbing dreams, I destroy your works now in the name of Jesus. Your power is broken, and your influence is nullified.

Father, Your Word says that You have not given me the spirit of fear, but of sonship, to cry "Abba Father." Lord, I cry out to You today to deliver me from the fear of evil dreams in the name of Jesus. I release the fire of God to consume every ancestral or generational connection to evil dreams in my life.

By the power of the Holy Spirit, I break every covenant, every agreement with evil, and every chain that the enemy has used to bind me or my family. I overcome every family and ancestral stronghold by the Blood of Jesus Christ. I pull down every stronghold in my mind that has been created to influence my dreams.

I disconnect myself from every human satanic agent who has been sent to manipulate or influence my dreams. I take full authority over every cell, organ, and system of my body, and I forbid any oppressive spirit from having dominion over them in Jesus' name.

By the power of the Holy Spirit, I rebuke every marine spirit, every spiritual personality, and every evil entity assigned to attack my dream life. I nullify their influence, attacks, and manipulations right now, in the name of Jesus Christ.

From this moment forward, I declare that I am free from every evil force and negative influence. My dreams will be filled with peace, divine insight, and the presence of the Holy Spirit. I walk in divine protection, and the Blood of Jesus covers and secures my mind. In the mighty name of Jesus, I pray, Amen.

Prayer Eighteen

PRAYER FOR FAVOR AND WISDOM

Father, in the mighty name of Jesus, I come before You, asking for Your favor. I ask for favor with You and favor with all people. Grant me favors with my children, spouse, and relatives at home, work, and in the marketplace. Lord, let Your favor rest upon me with members of my fellowship, customers, and employer.

May Your goodness and mercy follow me all the days of my life, and may Your favor open doors no man can shut. I ask You to reveal the secrets in circumstances, situations, and motives, for nothing is hidden. Unravel every mystery in my life, Father, and give me understanding through dreams and visions.

Lord, restore my spiritual sight and remove veils that blur my vision. Open my eyes to see clearly and discern Your will. Father, reveal Your heart and speak to me through dreams, visions, and divine strategies. Show me how to overcome the obstacles placed by the enemy. Illuminate my path and make it shine as bright as the morning sun.

Your Word says, *"Call to Me, and I will show you great and mighty things which you do not know."* (Jeremiah 33:3)

Thank You for granting me access to Your throne room, Lord.

I praise You, Jehovah Rohi, my Shepherd, because You see and know all. Heal any spiritual blindness in me, and grant me a clean, discerning spiritual sight that cannot be deceived. Reveal any potential dangers, fraud, mischief, or disasters to me so that I can pray and avert them in Jesus' name.

Father, I trust that my entire life and destiny are in Your hands, and I know You can bring everything to pass according to Your will. I thank You in advance for answering my prayers.

Lord, I also ask for wisdom. Give me a wise and understanding heart, like Solomon's. Release insight and foresight upon me. Let wisdom flow like a river that cannot be contained or dried up. Teach me to walk, talk, live, and act wisely.

Help me guard my mind from error, my heart from evil thoughts, and my life from harmful actions. Release supernatural wisdom so I can walk through the open doors of favor that You have prepared for me. Strengthen my spirit with purity and fill me with the right thoughts and words for every situation—whether in exhortation, counseling, comfort, or encouragement.

I thank You, Lord, for the wisdom, favor, and understanding You pour out upon me. In Jesus' mighty name, I pray, Amen.

Prayer Nineteen

PRAYER FOR PROTECTION AND BLESSING OVER SCHOOL

Heavenly Father, I thank You for every superintendent, school board member, teacher, principal, counselor, staff member, and child in the school system. I lift them to You, asking for Your continued blessings and protection upon their lives. Cover each of them, Lord, from the crown of their heads to the soles of their feet, and let no weapon formed against them prosper in the name of Jesus. I come against every evil assignment targeting the schools and command it to be destroyed now in Jesus' name. I thank you for Godly employees. Cover the schools with the precious blood of Jesus Christ.

Father, I thank You for placing a hedge of protection around every school, and I ask that You dismantle every plan, plot, and scheme of the enemy. I decree a divine reversal of what the enemy meant for evil. I bind any violence, including mass shootings and terrorist attacks, in all schools. I speak peace over the minds of every staff member and student. I bind the spirit of suicide and addiction, along with all suicidal tendencies, in Jesus' name. Heal hearts and minds from trauma. I oppose mind confusion and mental intrusion. I bind peer pressure and self-destructive behaviors. Give the students a humble heart and an obedient spirit and guide them in wise decisions. I thank You, Father, for Your healing power. You are Jehovah Rapha, the God who heals. Release Your healing virtue in schools. Strengthen their immune system. I rebuke any demonic forces behind infirmities, outbreaks, epidemics, or pandemics. Let them come under the covering of Psalm 91:2—You are our refuge and fortress, and we trust in You. You have promised to deliver us in times of trouble, and I ask for Your mercy and protection over every school.

Father, release Your peace and the wind of Your Holy Spirit in all schools. Let the students experience productivity, accelerated learning, and above-average test scores. Thank You for Your divine intervention and protection, and I declare that Your presence will guide every step of their academic year.

In Jesus' mighty name, I pray, Amen.

Prayer Twenty

PRAYER FOR THE POWER OF SCRIPTURE IN PRAYER

The Scriptures provide us with the foundation of our prayers. When we declare God's promises, they hold power and will bring about the desired outcomes in our lives.

The Scriptures are the perfect prayer, for they will never return void. They will always accomplish the purpose for which they are sent. As it is written in Isaiah 55:11 (The Voice): *"So it is when I declare something. My word will go out and not return to Me empty, but it will do what I wanted; it will accomplish what I determined."*

As we declare God's promises, they hold power and will bring about the desired outcomes in our lives.

Psalm 91 (The Voice Bible) reminds us of God's protection and care:

1. He who takes refuge in the shelter of the Most High will be safe in the shadow of the Almighty.

2. He will say to the Eternal, "My shelter, my mighty fortress, my God, I place all my trust in You."

3. For He will rescue you from the snares set by your enemies who entrap you and from deadly plagues.

4. Like a bird protecting its young, God will cover you with His feathers, will protect you under His great wings; His faithfulness will form a shield around you, a rock-solid wall to protect you.

5. You will not dread the terrors that haunt the night or enemy arrows that fly in the day, nor the plagues that lurk in darkness or the disasters that wreak havoc at noon.

6. A thousand may fall on your left, ten thousand may die on your right, but these horrors won't come near you.

7. Only your eyes will witness the punishment that awaits the evil, but you will not suffer because of it.

8. For you made the Eternal your refuge, the Most High your only home.

9. No evil will come to you; plagues will be turned away at your door.

10. He will command His heavenly messengers to guard you, to keep you safe in every way.

11. They will hold you up in their hands so that you will not crash, or fall, or even graze your foot on a stone.

12. You will walk on the lion and the cobra; you will trample the lion and the serpent underfoot.

13. "Because he clings to Me in love, I will rescue him from harm; I will set him above danger. Because he has known Me

by name, he will call on Me, and I will answer. I'll be with him through hard times; I'll rescue him and grant him honor. I'll reward him with many good years on this earth and let him witness My salvation."

Psalm 23 (The Voice Bible) further assures us of God's constant presence and provision:

1. The Eternal is my shepherd; He cares for me always.

2. He provides me rest in rich, green fields beside streams of refreshing water. He soothes my fears.

3. He makes me whole again, steering me off worn, hard paths to roads where truth and righteousness echo His name.

4. Even in the unending shadows of death's darkness, I am not overcome by fear. Because You are with me in those dark moments, near with Your protection and guidance, I am comforted.

5. You spread out a table before me, provisions in the midst of attack from my enemies; You care for all my needs, anointing my head with soothing, fragrant oil, filling my cup again and again with Your grace.

6. Certainly, Your faithful protection and loving provision will pursue me wherever I go, always, everywhere. I will always be with the Eternal, in Your house forever.

Prayer Twenty-One

PRAYER FOR CLARITY AND PURPOSE

Heavenly Father, I refuse to be distracted by insignificant things or people. Every agenda set to hinder and frustrate my assignment ceases in the name of Jesus. I boldly declare that I am walking in my God-given purpose.

Thank You, Father, for allowing me to be your child and securing my citizenship in heaven. I pray that I will willingly submit to the work of the Holy Spirit. Even when I don't fully understand, I trust Your perfect plan for my life.

Help me fulfill all that You have called me to do without hesitation. I put my hands on the plow and will not look back. Thank You for surrounding me with like-minded individuals who walk in harmony and love. Thank You for the anointing of being jointly fit and for connecting me with those who will help me accomplish my kingdom assignment.

I call forth every individual and resource assigned to help me fulfill my mandate during this season. I declare that anyone or anything hindering my progress must move out of my sphere of influence now.

I thank You, Father, that everything in my life flows unhindered and uncontaminated. Every blockage is removed, and I now experience overflow in every area of my life. I thank You for the fresh wind, fire, and strength for the journey ahead. In Jesus' name, we pray. Amen.

Prayer Twenty-Two

PRAYER FOR FREEDOM FROM ANXIETY AND FEAR

Heavenly Father, I place every fear and anxiety at Your feet. Help me eliminate all doubts and fears when I feel overwhelmed. Father, remind me that I can always trust in You. Your Word says, *"Cast your cares upon the Lord, for He cares for you."* (1 Peter 5:7). I refuse to worry and instead choose to trust You. I refuse to fret, panic, or be consumed by my present circumstances. You, O Lord, are the strength of my life—of whom shall I be afraid?

I repent for opening the door to the spirits of fear, anxiety, and stress in my family line and for anything I've done through sin or association. Father, wash me clean with the precious blood of Jesus Christ and remove these spirits from my spirit, soul, body, memory, and mind. As Your offspring and joint heir with Christ, I take authority over all powers of the enemy. I rebuke and break every stronghold of fear, anxiety, and stress, and I lose myself from these spirits in the mighty name of Jesus.

I break and loose myself from all emotional attachments to fear, anxiety, and stress. I cast these spirits into the abyss, never to return, in Jesus' name. I decree that the peace of God will guard my heart and mind as I focus on Christ. I welcome the Holy Spirit to replace the presence of fear, stress, and anxiety and invite His peace, joy, and righteousness to fill my heart.

Lord, flood my heart with Your peace that surpasses all understanding and fills me with unspeakable joy.

I declare that the strongholds of worry, fear, and anxiety will crumble and be permanently destroyed.

In Jesus' name, I command and cast out every spirit of anxiety, palpitations, headaches, fatigue, emotional stress, phobias, post-traumatic stress, and obsessive-compulsive behaviors. I command these spirits to go to the abyss, never to return.

Thank You, Lord, for replacing fear with peace and anxiety with joy. In Jesus' mighty name, we pray.

Amen.

Prayer Twenty-Three

MIND CONTROL PRAYER

Lord, I come before You, asking for healing in the land of my mind and heart. I command my mind to be sound right now, and I cast out every distraction in the mighty name of Jesus. Lord, take control of my thoughts and take them captive. Reveal all that needs to be healed and bring restoration to my mind and soul.

I break and cancel all word curses spoken over me in the name of Jesus. Father, I repent and renounce all forms of mind control, as well as all generational sins and curses of iniquity. I cancel every generational curse and bind the powers of mind-control demons in the mighty name of Jesus.

I renounce every legal ground that allows mind-control demons to operate in my life, and I break their hold over me now in the name of Jesus. I bind and break all mind-controlling and mind-binding demons, and I order them to lose their grip over me now. I command every mind-controlling spirit to come up and out and go in Jesus' mighty name.

Mind control, I sever your tentacles now in Jesus' name. Every demonic attachment to my mind and body is cut off, and I break your hold in the name of Jesus. I command every evil spirit operating through mind control to lose me and leave now, in Jesus' name.

Let the fire of God consume every demonic spirit and every

stronghold. I break all demonic spirits that work with mind-control spirits, and I command them to go now in the name of Jesus.

I declare the power of God's Word over my mind right now. I plead the blood of Jesus over my mind, and I declare that I have the mind of Christ. I speak clarity and stability to my thoughts—my mind is clear and free from confusion in Jesus' name. I declare that my mind is pure, filled with godly thoughts, and aligned with God's will.

I have godly love in my heart and mind. The Word of God transforms my mind, and I agree with His truth. I love the Lord with all my heart, mind, and soul.

All demonic powers are destroyed now in the name of Jesus. I command every spirit of confusion, panic, anxiety, mental breakdown, and self-harm to go now in the name of Jesus Christ.

I order every demon wrapped around my spine to uncoil and come out now in the name of Jesus. I break every chain of witchcraft, sorcery, and pride, and I command them to go now. I cast out all unsound doctrine and false teachings and break all word curses spoken over me.

Thank You, Jesus, for setting me free. Holy Spirit, fill me with Your presence to overflow and restore my mind, body, and spirit. In Jesus' name, Amen.

Prayer Twenty-Four

PRAYER FOR THE YOUTH

Heavenly Father, I come, asking for Your divine intervention in the lives of our youth. We bind the negative influences of this world and declare that our children will see themselves as You see them. I command every evil assignment against them to be destroyed in the mighty name of Jesus.

Pour out Your Spirit upon them, Lord. Let them perceive themselves through the lens of the Holy Spirit. I declare that our children shall be spiritually and naturally educated, equipped with wisdom from You.

Father, I pray they will personally encounter You, the One who can transform everything. Grant them a spirit of wisdom and revelation so they may understand the mysteries and secrets hidden in their deep and intimate knowledge of You. Open their eyes, hearts, and ears in a way that only You can, Lord.

May our children come to know and understand the calling You've placed upon their lives, the inheritance You've given them, and the purpose You've positioned them for in this very moment. I ask that Your grace and mercy be poured into their lives and that the Holy Spirit moves powerfully in their hearts.

Reveal Yourself to the next generation, Father, so they may

personally experience Your power and glory. Let them know the greatness of Your anointing, wisdom, and presence. We thank You, Lord, that our children are the future. Let them be the light in a dark world. They will have influence and affluence.

I place a shield of protection around them, Father. Let Your favor surround them as a shield. Grant them Holy Ghost boldness, that they may lead and not follow, be first and not last. We declare that every chain of bondage that seeks to hold them will be broken in Jesus' name.

I pray You would shine the light on every dark situation surrounding our youth. Satan, you cannot have our children. I take authority over every work of darkness and declare victory for our young people.

Father, I also lift the educators and all personnel shaping our children's lives. Cover teachers, administrators, counselors, cafeteria workers, janitors, students, and all staff. We plead the blood of Jesus over each school and each person and ask that Your protection and guidance be upon them all.

Give pastors and spiritual leaders worldwide fresh ideas and new avenues to reach and influence children, drawing them closer to You. Grant them divine wisdom for this time and in this age so that they may lead our youth into a deeper relationship with You.

In the mighty name of Jesus, we pray. Amen.

Prayer Twenty-Five

PREPARATION AND
HEALTH PROTOCOL

My Savior,

I come before You, asking for Your preparation for what lies ahead.

Help me die to my flesh and become anchored in You. Father, change my appetite and remove cravings for sugars, carbohydrates, and anything harmful to my health. Guide me with the protocol for my health so that I may live and not die, And declare the works of the Lord.

Lord, let me crave only those things that benefit my body foods that fuel me and make me feel vibrant. I want to renew my mind regarding my nutritional choices and give myself a clear path to a healthy lifestyle. I thank you that my body is in homeostasis balance.

I ask for a regimen of exercise that strengthens and empowers my body. Bless and cover everything I eat and drink, according to Your Word in Mark 16:18, which says, *"They shall take up serpents; and if they drink any deadly thing, it shall not hurt them; They shall lay hands on the sick, and they shall recover."*

Strengthen my immune system and purge all harmful pathogens and viruses. Every system in my body functions the way God intended it to. Fortify my body to fight against anything that threatens me. Shut down every demonic agenda that seeks to harm me.

Lord, take away my desire for the things I don't need. Show me the diet for my destiny that aligns with Your purpose and plan for my life.

In Jesus' name, I pray.
Amen.

Prayer Twenty-Six

PRAYER FOR DISCERNMENT

Father, I come before You, asking You to heighten my discernment. In Matthew 24:24, Your Word declares, *"For there shall arise false Christs, and false prophets, and shall show great signs and wonders; so much so that, if it were possible, they would deceive the very elect."* Lord, help me to discern the spirits around me and protect me from deception.

Remove anything or anyone from my life that causes weariness, distractions, or confusion. Connect me with those in the fivefold ministry who will help sharpen my spiritual discernment and provide me with the guidance and support I need on this journey.

I declare that the mantle of discernment rests upon me. Stretch forth Your scepter over every situation I encounter, granting me the wisdom and authority to act upon what You reveal to me. I thank You for empowering me to see into the spirit realm and understand the darkness and the light.

I will not fear the revelations You give me, even in dark places, for You have given me power over all the forces of darkness. Thank You, Jesus, for revealing things through my five senses.

I commit to operating with unwavering spiritual integrity in my discernment, resisting the temptation to delve into things You have not yet allowed to be revealed.

Lord, let information and revelation flow through teaching, and let discernment be activated. I declare that I will not be ignorant of the enemy's devices. I will keenly detect the wiles of darkness and stand firm in the power and authority You have given me, constantly vigilant and empowered.

In Jesus' name, I pray. Amen.

Prayer Twenty-Seven

PRAYER COVERED UNDER THE BLOOD OF JESUS

Heavenly Father,

I come before You in the mighty name of Jesus, the Lamb of God, whose blood was shed for my sins. I thank You for the gift of salvation, the sacrifice of Jesus, and the power of His blood that cleanses, heals, and protects.

Lord, I apply the precious blood of Jesus over my life today. I declare that the blood of Jesus covers me, my family, my home, my work, and all that I hold dear. May His blood speak for me in every circumstance, silencing the accuser's voice and bringing peace into my heart.

By the blood of Jesus, I am redeemed from the curse of sin and death. I thank You, Lord, for Your grace and mercy. I claim the power of the blood to break every chain of addiction, fear, and oppression in my life. I declare that no weapon formed against me shall prosper, for the blood of Jesus shields me.

Father, I ask for the healing power of Jesus' blood to flow over me now. May His stripes bring healing to every area of my life—physical, emotional, and spiritual. I declare that by His blood, I am made whole.

I also pray for protection today. Cover me under the blood of Jesus, Lord. Keep me safe from harm, sickness, evil, and anything that seeks to destroy me. I place my trust in Your covering, knowing that the blood of Jesus is my defense and victory.

I surrender my will to You, Lord, and I thank You for the assurance that through the blood of Jesus, I am made new. Help me to live in the fullness of what He has done for me, walking in the authority and grace He has provided.

In Jesus' mighty name,
Amen.

Prayer Twenty-Eight

PRAYER FOR SPIRITUAL LEADERS

Father, I thank You for pastors and spiritual leaders around the world. I ask that You give them divine ideas and new avenues to influence children and lead them to You. Grant them wisdom for this time and age, that they may shepherd with discernment and purpose.

I lift every pastor, spiritual leader, and all who serve in the fivefold ministry. You have said that the feet of those who carry the gospel are beautiful. Lord, let them stand strong and unshaken in the face of the pressures of this world. Keep their bodies healthy and their minds sound.

Strengthen them from the crown of their heads to the soles of their feet. Grant them supernatural favor and uncommon grace. Reestablish the sound of holiness in their hearts and ministries. As Your Word declares in 1 Timothy 5:17, *"The elders who direct the affairs of the church well are worthy of double honor, especially those whose work is preaching and teaching."* Father, may they be counted worthy of this calling and fulfill all the good pleasure of Your will with the work of faith and power.

Let Your Word have a free course in their lives, Father. I ask that You give them the spirit of wisdom and revelation in the knowledge of Jesus. Enlighten the eyes of their understanding so that they may know the hope of their calling and the exceeding greatness of Your power toward those who believe.

Strengthen them with might by Your Spirit in their inner being. Let Christ dwell in their hearts through faith; may they be rooted and grounded in Your love. Help them comprehend the breadth, length, depth, and height of Your love with all saints, which surpasses all understanding.

May Your love always bring peace to their hearts. I receive multiplied grace and peace for them as they contend for the faith. Cover and protect their families, Lord, and provide for all their needs. Bless them abundantly and prosper them, giving them the desires of their hearts. I bind every distraction and time-waster, and I declare that every agenda meant to hinder, dilute, compromise, or persecute those who preach the gospel of Jesus Christ will be judged in the mighty name of Jesus.

Renew and refresh Your leaders, O Lord, releasing fresh wind and fire. Grant them strength for the journey, and equip them with the endurance to continue faithfully in the work You've called them to.

I pray all of this in the precious name of Jesus. Amen.

Prayer Twenty-Nine

PRAYER TO APPLY THE BLOOD OF JESUS OVER MY PROPERTY

Father God, I come before You in the mighty name of Jesus Christ, putting on the whole armor You have provided to stand firm against the enemy's schemes. I acknowledge that my struggle is not against flesh and blood but against the rulers, authorities, and powers of this dark world and the spiritual forces of evil in the heavenly realms (Ephesians 6:12). I clothe myself with the full armor of God and ask for the gift of discernment and wisdom from Your Holy Spirit.

I cover my home and all that is within it under the precious blood of Jesus. I declare that only the Holy Spirit is allowed to dwell here. I invite the Holy Spirit to be present in every room, leading and guiding my family and me in Your truth and filling this space with peace, protection, and divine order.

I call upon Your angels to assist us, to war on our behalf, and to drive out any evil spirits that may be present. In the name of Jesus, I command every evil spirit to leave my house now! You have no place here, and you must go. I command the spirit of infirmity to depart. I command every occult spirit, every serpent spirit, every monitoring spirit, every Pharaoh spirit, every Python spirit, every Leviathan spirit, and every spirit of pride, rebellion, and rejection to leave in the name of Jesus.

I place the fire of God upon the heads of every witch and warlock, and I declare that no weapon formed against us shall prosper. I close every door and window in the spiritual realm that may serve as an entry point for evil spirits. From this moment forward, my home is sealed, and no demonic power will have access here.

I decree that only angels assigned by the Commander of Heaven's armies can enter this home. I apply the blood of Jesus over every door, every window, and every entry point as a sign to all spirits that the blood of Jesus covers this house. I declare that evil spirits must pass over this house and never enter again, in the name of Jesus.

I ask You, Lord, to reveal any items in this home that may serve as a gateway for evil spirits. I repent and remove any spiritually contaminated objects, renouncing their influence. I close every spiritual doorway and entry point the enemy has used to gain access to this home. I seal these access points with the precious blood of Jesus, and I declare them closed and sealed forever.

Thank You, Lord, for Your protection and cleansing. I trust in Your power to safeguard my home and property from all evil. The blood of Jesus covers, protects, and shields us. In His mighty name, I pray.

Amen.

Prayer Thirty

PRAYER OF RESTORATION

Lord, I come before You today, claiming the promise of Joel 2:25-26: *"I will restore to you the years that the locusts have eaten."* Father, you are the God of restoration, and I trust in Your ability to renew and restore all things.

I bring before You every area of my life that needs healing and restoration. I ask You to restore my spirit, relationships, health, finances, and every part of me that has been broken, wounded, or torn. You are the One who binds up the brokenhearted, and I know that You can heal and renew every place of hurt and loss in my life.

I lay before You my feelings of disappointment, regret, and failure. I know that You, Lord, can bring beauty from ashes. Restore my hope, my joy, and my peace. Renew my strength, as You have promised, and give me the courage to keep moving forward, even when the way ahead is unclear. Help me trust in Your perfect timing and unending love, knowing that You will lead me through.

Lord, I also ask You to restore my relationships—whether with family, friends, or others. Heal any divisions, hurts, or misunderstandings. Bring reconciliation where there has been strife, and let Your peace reign in every connection. Help me forgive, let go of past offenses, and allow proper healing in my heart and relationships.

I declare that what the enemy has tried to steal from me, you will return sevenfold. I trust that Your plans for me are good and that You will restore not just what I've lost but will bless me abundantly, beyond what I could ever imagine.

Father, I thank You for Your power of restoration. I believe that nothing is too broken for You to heal and restore. I surrender every area of my life into Your loving hands and declare that Your perfect will shall be done in my life.

In Jesus' mighty name, I pray. Amen.

Stay Connected

 www.Facebook.com/Sister2SisterOneHeart

 www.instagram.com/jennifer01_

 jennifermclean74@gmail.com

PRAYERS FOR THE
GOOD FIGHT

Persistent Faith in Action

JENNIFER MCLEAN

Made in the USA
Columbia, SC
01 July 2025

60086574R00041